"It's hard to connect with your child without first understanding where they are. As counselors and speakers at parenting events across the country, we spend a great deal of time teaching parents about development. To know *where* your child is—not just physically, but emotionally, socially, and spiritually, helps you to truly know and understand *who* your child is. And that understanding is the key to connecting. The Phase Guides give you the tools to do just that. Our wise friends Reggie and Kristen have put together an insightful, hopeful, practical, and literal year-by-year guide that will help you to understand and connect with your child at every age."

SISSY GOFF
M.ED., LPC-MHSP, DIRECTOR OF CHILD & ADOLESCENT COUNSELING AT DAYSTAR COUNSELING MINISTRIES IN NASHVILLE, TENNESSEE, SPEAKER AND AUTHOR OF ARE MY KIDS ON TRACK?

"These resources for parents are fantastically empowering, absolute in their simplicity, and completely doable in every way. The hard work that has gone into the Phase Project will echo through the next generation of children in powerful ways."

JENNIFER WALKER
RN BSN, AUTHOR AND FOUNDER OF MOMS ON CALL

"We all know where we want to end up in our parenting, but how to get there can seem like an unsolved mystery. Through the Phase Project series, Reggie Joiner and Kristen Ivy team up to help us out. The result is a resource that guides us through the different seasons of raising children, and provides a road map to parenting in such a way that we finish up with very few regrets."

SANDRA STANLEY
FOSTER CARE ADVOCATE, BLOGGER, WIFE TO ANDY STANLEY, MOTHER OF THREE

"Not only are the Phase Guides the most creative and well-thought-out guides to parenting I have ever encountered, these books are ESSENTIAL to my daily parenting. With a 13-year-old, 11-year-old, and 9-year-old at home, I am swimming in their wake of daily drama and delicacy. These books are a reminder to enjoy every second. Because it's just a phase."

CARLOS WHITTAKER
AUTHOR, SPEAKER, FATHER OF THREE

"As the founder of Minnie's Food Pantry, I see thousands of people each month with children who will benefit from the advice, guidance, and nuggets of information on how to celebrate and understand the phases of their child's life. Too often we feel like we're losing our mind when sweet little Johnny starts to change his behavior into a person we do not know. I can't wait to start implementing the principles of these books with my clients to remind them . . . it's just a phase."

CHERYL JACKSON
FOUNDER OF MINNIE'S FOOD PANTRY, AWARD-WINNING PHILANTHROPIST, AND GRANDMOTHER

"I began exploring this resource with my counselor hat on, thinking how valuable this will be for the many parents I spend time with in my office. I ended up taking my counselor hat off and putting on my parent hat. Then I kept thinking about friends who are teachers, coaches, youth pastors, and children's ministers, who would want this in their hands. What a valuable resource the Orange team has given us to better understand and care for the kids and adolescents we love. I look forward to sharing it broadly."

DAVID THOMAS
LMSW, DIRECTOR OF FAMILY COUNSELING, DAYSTAR COUNSELING MINISTRIES, SPEAKER AND AUTHOR OF ARE MY KIDS ON TRACK? *AND* WILD THINGS: THE ART OF NURTURING BOYS

"I have always wished someone would hand me a manual for parenting. Well, the Phase Guides are more than what I wished for. They guide, inspire, and challenge me as a parent—while giving me incredible insight into my children at each age and phase. Our family will be using these every year!"

COURTNEY DEFEO
AUTHOR OF IN THIS HOUSE, WE WILL GIGGLE, *MOTHER OF TWO*

"As I speak to high school students and their parents, I always wonder to myself: What would it have been like if they had better seen what was coming next? What if they had a guide that would tell them what to expect and how to be ready? What if they could anticipate what is predictable about the high school years before they actually hit? These Phase Guides give a parent that kind of preparation so they can have a plan when they need it most."

JOSH SHIPP
AUTHOR, TEEN EXPERT, AND YOUTH SPEAKER

"The Phase Guides are incredibly creative, well researched, and filled with inspirational actions for everyday life. Each age-specific guide is catalytic for equipping parents to lead and love their kids as they grow up. I'm blown away and deeply encouraged by the content and by its creators. I highly recommend Phase resources for all parents, teachers, and influencers of children. This is the stuff that challenges us and changes our world. Get them. Read them. And use them!"

DANIELLE STRICKLAND
OFFICER WITH THE SALVATION ARMY, AUTHOR, SPEAKER, MOTHER OF TWO

"It's true that parenting is one of life's greatest joys but it is not without its challenges. If we're honest, parenting can sometimes feel like trying to choreograph a dance to an ever-changing beat. It can be clumsy and riddled with well-meaning missteps. If parenting is a dance, this Parenting Guide is a skilled instructor refining your technique and helping you move gracefully to a steady beat. For those of us who love to plan ahead, this guide will help you anticipate what's to come so you can be poised and ready to embrace the moments you want to enjoy."

TINA NAIDOO
MSSW, LCSW EXECUTIVE DIRECTOR, THE POTTER'S HOUSE OF DALLAS, INC.

PARENTING YOUR TWO-YEAR-OLD

A GUIDE TO MAKING THE MOST OF THE "I CAN DO IT" PHASE

KRISTEN IVY AND REGGIE JOINER

PARENTING YOUR TWO-YEAR-OLD
A GUIDE TO MAKING THE MOST OF THE
"I CAN DO IT" PHASE

Published by Orange, a division of The reThink Group, Inc.,
5870 Charlotte Lane, Suite 300,
Cumming, GA 30040 U.S.A.

©2017 Kristen Ivy and Reggie Joiner
Authors: Kristen Ivy and Reggie Joiner
Lead Editor: Karen Wilson
Editing Team: Melanie Williams, Hannah Crosby, Sherry Surratt

Art Direction: Ryan Boon and Hannah Crosby
Book Design: FiveStone and Sharon van Rossum

Printed in the United States of America
First Edition 2017
1 2 3 4 5 6 7 8 9 10

Special thanks to:

Jim Burns, Ph.D for guidance and consultation
on having conversations about sexual integrity

Jon Acuff for guidance and consultation on having
conversations about technological responsibility

Jean Sumner, MD for guidance and consultation
on having conversations about healthy habits

Every educator, counselor, community leader, and
researcher who invested in the Phase Project

TABLE OF CONTENTS

HOW TO USE THIS GUIDE .... pg. 9

WELCOME TO A NEW PHASE .... pg. 10

52 WEEKS
TO PARENT YOUR TWO-YEAR-OLD .... pg. 13

pg. 14 **MEASURE YOUR WEEKS**   pg. 22 **DISCOVER THIS PHASE**

SIX THINGS
EVERY KID NEEDS .... pg. 31

pg. 34 **LOVE**
ONE QUESTION YOUR
TWO-YEAR-OLD IS ASKING

pg. 52 **FUN**
WAYS TO HAVE FUN
WITH YOUR TWO-YEAR-OLD

pg. 40 **STORIES**
BOOKS TO READ
TO YOUR TWO-YEAR-OLD

pg. 58 **PEOPLE**
ADULTS WHO MIGHT INFLUENCE
YOUR TWO-YEAR-OLD

pg. 46 **WORK**
WORK YOUR
TWO-YEAR-OLD CAN DO

pg. 64 **WORDS**
WORDS YOUR TWO-YEAR-OLD
NEEDS TO HEAR

FOUR CONVERSATIONS
TO HAVE IN THIS PHASE .... pg. 71

pg. 74 **HEALTH**
ESTABLISH BASIC NUTRITION

pg. 86 **TECHNOLOGY**
ENJOY THE ADVANTAGES

pg. 80 **SEX**
INTRODUCE THEM
TO THEIR BODY

pg. 92 **FAITH**
INCITE THEIR SENSE
OF WONDER

THE RHYTHM OF YOUR WEEK .... pg. 98

PHASE LIFE MAP OVERVIEW .... pg. 106

HOW TO USE THIS ~~BOOK~~ ~~JOURNAL~~ GUIDE

The guide you hold in your hand doesn't have very many words, but it does have a lot of ideas. Some of these ideas come from thousands of hours of research. Others come from parents, educators, and volunteers who spend every day with kids the same age as yours. This guide won't tell you everything about your kid, but it will tell you a few things about kids at this age.

The best way to use this guide is to take what these pages tell you about toddlers and combine it with what you know is true about your toddler.

Let's sum it up:

THINGS ABOUT TODDLERS +
THOUGHTS ABOUT *YOUR* TODDLER =
YOUR GUIDE TO THE NEXT 52 WEEKS OF PARENTING

After each idea in this guide, there are pages with a few questions designed to prompt you to think about your kid, your family, and yourself as a parent. The only guarantee we give to parents who use this guide is this: You will mess up some things as a parent this year. Actually, that's a guarantee to every parent, regardless. But you, you picked up this book! You want to be a better parent. And that's what we hope this guide will do: help you parent your toddler just a little better, simply because you paused to consider a few ideas that can help you make the most of this phase.

THE TWO-YEAR-OLD PHASE

Life can be challenging and unpredictable. And, if you're parenting a two-year-old, you're guaranteed this year will have plenty of both. That sweet baby who used to cuddle in your arms has not only learned how to walk, but now he can run away from you—*and fast.* That little angel whose smile used to light up your world can now smile at you as she drops your phone—*into the bathtub.*

Personally, I've raised two men who have given me four beautiful grandchildren all currently under the age of six years old. I've seen enough to know the phrase "terrible twos" wasn't invented without reason. There are days in this phase when "terrible" may seem like the only word to characterize the state of your home, your schedule, and your patience. This is the phase when a toddler suddenly explodes with personality.

It's the moment they fall to the floor screaming because you cut their sandwich the wrong way. Or you bring them the milk they asked for, and they realize they really wanted orange juice. Or you tell them they aren't allowed to do that completely irrational thing they were just trying to do, and the world suddenly falls apart. Yes, you will have moments this year when you stare, wide-eyed, at the determined child in front of you and wonder: *What am I supposed to do with this?*

The answer, even though it may not seem true in the moment, is really what it has always been: love. Becoming a grandparent has heightened my senses to my grandchildren's need for love. It's funny, the way time gives us perspective. Love is the thing every selfish, stubborn, crazy-headed toddler needs most.

I remember when my grandson Amari was two he told me he loved me for the first time. Each time he said it, he put his whole body into it. It was like he couldn't say it loud enough or strong enough. He just had to let me know that HE LOVED ME!

One day, as I was leaving his house, we started a back-and-forth shouting match to tell each other how much we loved each other. It was so passionate and so pure that I took out my cell phone and recorded him on video. Within days after sharing it on social media, over 26 million people had watched, commented, and shared the video. The video was shown on *Good Morning America* and *The Ellen Show*.

I know most people's toddler videos don't make national television. But that's not the point. The point is there's something about the love of a two-year-old that can capture the heart of a nation. And that love is inside your child, too.

Sure, this year your toddler is becoming more independent. But that means when she shows you love and affection, she does it because she chooses to. When he tells you he loves you, he says it because *he means it*. And as the parent of a two-year-old, you'll discover you have more love inside you than you ever knew possible. It's a shouting-match kind of love that will see you through the tantrums. It's a love that may catch you off guard as you find yourself captivated by this adorable, growing, bundle of personality.

- CHERYL JACKSON
FOUNDER OF MINNIE'S FOOD PANTRY, AWARD-WINNING PHILANTHROPIST, AND GRANDMOTHER

SECTION ONE

—

52 WEEKS

TO PARENT YOUR

TWO-YEAR-OLD

WHEN YOU SEE
HOW MUCH

Time

YOU HAVE LEFT

—

YOU TEND TO DO

More

WITH THE TIME
YOU HAVE NOW.

THERE ARE APPROXIMATELY

936 WEEKS

FROM THE TIME A BABY IS BORN
UNTIL THEY GROW UP AND MOVE TO
WHATEVER IS NEXT.

It may seem hard to believe, but at least 104 of those weeks have already passed you by. And, while the future still feels far away, you're probably beginning to realize that your toddler is growing up faster than you ever dreamed.

That's why every week counts. Of course, each week on its own might not feel significant. There may be weeks this year when you feel like all you've accomplished was enduring an epic toddler tantrum. That's okay.

Take a deep breath.
You don't have to get everything done this week.

But what happens in your child's life week after week, year after year, adds up over time. So, it might be a good idea to put a number to your weeks.

MEASURE IT OUT.

Write down the number of weeks that have already passed since your toddler was born. Then write down the number of weeks you have left before they graduate high school.

HINT: If you want a little help counting it out, you can download the free Parent Cue app on all mobile platforms.

_____

_____

_____

CREATE A VISUAL COUNTDOWN.

 Find a jar and fill it with one marble for each week you have remaining with your child. Then make a habit of removing one marble every week as a reminder to make the most of your time you have with your child.

Where can you place your visual countdown so you will see it frequently?

_____

_____

_____

_____

Which day of the week is best for you to remove a marble?

_____

_____

_____

Is there anything you want to do each week as you remove a marble? (*Examples: say a prayer, write in a baby book, retell one favorite memory from this past week*)

_____

_____

_____

_____

_____

_____

_____

_____

_____

_____

_____

_____

EVERY PHASE IS A
TIMEFRAME
IN A KID'S LIFE
WHEN YOU CAN
LEVERAGE
DISTINCTIVE
OPPORTUNITIES
TO INFLUENCE
THEIR

future.

YOU ONLY HAVE
52 WEEKS
WITH YOUR TWO-YEAR-OLD

while they are still two.

Then they will be three,

and you will never know them as a two-year-old again.

That might be incredibly emotional,

or it might be the best news you've heard all day.

Or to say it another way:

Before you know it, your toddler will grow up a little more and . . .

be potty trained.

speak clearly.

blow their own nose.

Just remember, the phase you are in now has remarkable potential. Before their third birthday, there are some distinctive opportunities you don't want to miss. So, as you count down the next 52 weeks, pay attention to what makes these weeks different from the rest of the weeks you will have with your child as they grow.

What are some things you have noticed about your two-year-old in this phase that you really enjoy?

What is something new you are learning as a parent during this phase?

_____

_____

_____

_____

_____

_____

_____

_____

_____

_____

_____

_____

_____

_____

_____

_____

_____

TWO

—

THE PHASE WHEN NOBODY'S ON TIME, EVERYTHING'S A MESS, AND ONE EAGER TODDLER WILL INSIST,

"I can do it."

EXPECT TO BE LATE.

Maybe you had to wait for your toddler to "do it myself" (just try and stop them). Or maybe they impressively filled a clean diaper just as you got into the car. Whatever the reason, this phase will make even the most punctual adult miss the mark occasionally.

LOOK FORWARD TO A FEW FASHION STATEMENTS.

Expect a few mismatched outfits, magic marker tattoos, sticker collages, and other various states of creative expression. In this phase, you will choose not only your battles, but also which messes will just have to be tolerated.

THEIR STRUGGLE FOR INDEPENDENCE HAS BEGUN.

Your first clue might be your toddler's three new favorite words: "me," "myself," and "I." Just remember, by letting them do some things "myself," they're not only learning new skills, they're also developing the confidence they need in order to move to the next phase.

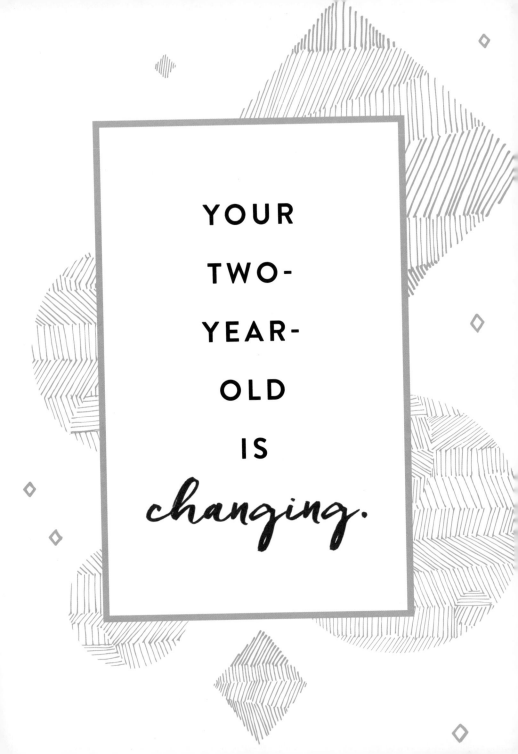

YOUR

TWO-

YEAR-

OLD

IS

changing.

PHYSICALLY

- Jumps in place
- Throws a ball overhead
- Briefly stands on one foot
- May demonstrate hand preference

VERBALLY

- Says 40-50 words including some action words like, "Go" (2 years)
- Says approximately 300 words and simple sentences like "I do it." (2 ½ years)
- Learns how to whisper (2 ½ years)
- Understands more than they can communicate

MENTALLY

- Follows simple instructions
- Benefits from repetition
- Is unable to take the point of view of other people
- Learns through engaging their five senses

EMOTIONALLY

- May begin to bite, scream, and throw tantrums
- Plays next to, rather than with, playmates
- Recognizes basic emotions in others
- May begin to name their own emotions like, "I'm happy."

What are some changes you are noticing about your two-year-old?

_____

_____

_____

_____

_____

_____

_____

You may disagree with some of the characteristics we've shared about two-year-olds. That's because every two-year-old is unique. What makes your two-year-old different from two-year-olds in general?

_____

_____

_____

_____

_____

_____

_____

_____

What do you want to remember about this year with your two-year-old?

Mark this page. Throughout the year, write down a few simple things that you want to remember. If you want to be really thorough, there are about 52 blank lines. But some weeks, you may be restocking the Cheerios® and milk and miss out on writing down a memory. That's okay.

_____

_____

_____

_____

_____

_____

_____

_____

_____

_____

_____

_____

_____

_____

_____

_____

_____

_____

_____

_____

_____

_____

_____

_____

_____

_____

_____

_____

_____

_____

_____

_____

SECTION TWO

SIX THINGS

EVERY KID

NEEDS

YOUR KID NEEDS **6** THINGS OVER TIME

LOVE

STORIES

WORDS

WORK

PEOPLE

FUN

OVER THE NEXT 832 WEEKS, YOUR CHILD WILL NEED MANY THINGS.

Some of the things your kid needs will change from phase to phase, but there are six things that every kid needs at every phase. In fact, these things may be the most important things you give your kid—other than food. Kids need food.

EVERY KID, AT EVERY PHASE, NEEDS . . .

♡ LOVE
to give them a sense of WORTH.

📖 STORIES
to give them a bigger PERSPECTIVE.

🏋 WORK
to give them PURPOSE.

♟ FUN
to give them CONNECTION.

👥 PEOPLE
to give them BELONGING.

💬 WORDS
to give them DIRECTION.

The next few pages are designed to help you think about how you will give these things to your two-year-old—before they turn three.

EVERY KID

NEEDS

love

OVER TIME

—

TO GIVE THEM

A SENSE OF

worth.

 ONE QUESTION YOUR TWO-YEAR-OLD IS ASKING

Your toddler's changing ability is a crisis—for you, and for them. This is a season filled with uncertainty, imperfection, and even failure as they struggle to keep up with all their newly developing skills.

Your two-year-old is asking one major question:

"AM I ABLE?"

As the parent of a two-year-old who may scream more than you imagined, sleep less than you had hoped, or make more messes than you thought possible, you may feel overwhelmed at times. But remember this—in order to give your two-year-old the love they need, you really only need to do one thing:

EMBRACE their physical needs.

When you embrace your toddler's physical needs, you . . .
communicate that they are safe,
establish that the world can be trusted,
and demonstrate that they are worth loving.

You are probably doing more than you realize to show your two-year-old just how much you love them. Make a list of the ways you already show up consistently to embrace their physical needs.

🏆 You may need to look at this list on a bad day to remember what a great parent you are.

_____

_____

_____

_____

_____

_____

_____

_____

_____

_____

_____

_____

_____

Showing love requires paying attention to what someone likes. What does your two-year-old seem to enjoy the most right now?

_____

_____

_____

_____

_____

_____

_____

_____

_____

_____

_____

_____

_____

_____

_____

_____

_____

_____

It's impossible to love anyone with the relentless effort a two-year-old demands unless you have a little time for yourself. What can you do to refuel each week so you are able to give your toddler the love they need?

_____

_____

_____

_____

_____

_____

_____

_____

_____

_____

_____

_____

_____

_____

_____

_____

Who do you have around you supporting you this year?

EVERY KID

NEEDS

stories

OVER TIME

—

TO GIVE THEM

A BIGGER

perspective.

BOOKS TO READ WITH YOUR TWO-YEAR OLD

FREIGHT TRAIN
by Donald Crews

LLAMA, LLAMA (SERIES)
by Anna Dewdney

EVERYONE POOPS
by Taro Gomi

IF YOU GIVE A MOUSE A COOKIE
by Laura Joffe Numeroff

THE SNOWY DAY
by Ezra Jack Keats

A FLY WENT BY
by Mike McClintock

BLUEBERRIES FOR SAL
by Robert McCloskey

ARE YOU MY MOTHER?
by P.D. Eastman

GO, DOG. GO!
by P.D. Eastman

DON'T LET THE PIGEON DRIVE THE BUS
by Mo Willems

THE FOOT BOOK
by Dr. Seuss

GOODNIGHT, GOODNIGHT, CONSTRUCTION SITE
by Sheri Duskey Rinker

LITTLE BLUE TRUCK
by Alice Schertle

WHERE THE WILD THINGS ARE
by Maurice Sendak

MR. BROWN CAN MOO! CAN YOU?
by Dr. Seuss

ONE FISH, TWO FISH, RED FISH, BLUE FISH
by Dr. Seuss

DUCK ON A BIKE
by David Shannon

SHEEP IN A JEEP
by Nancy E. Shaw

EVEN FIREFIGHTERS GO TO THE POTTY
by Wendy and Naomi Wax

Kids need the kind of stories you will read to them over time. But they also need family stories. What can you do this year to capture your family's story so you can retell the story of this year to your child when they are older?

_____

_____

_____

_____

_____

_____

_____

_____

_____

_____

_____

_____

_____

What makes your family history unique? How can you preserve the story of your family's history for your child?

_____

_____

_____

_____

_____

_____

_____

_____

_____

_____

_____

_____

_____

_____

_____

_____

_____

_____

_____

Are there other stories that matter to you? What are they, and how will you share those stories with your two-year-old?

_____

_____

_____

_____

_____

_____

_____

_____

_____

_____

_____

_____

_____

_____

_____

_____

_____

_____

WORK YOUR TWO-YEAR-OLD CAN DO

PICK UP A TOY AND PUT IT AWAY

HELP AS YOU DRESS THEM
(by holding out arms, legs, or feet)

HOLD A SIPPY CUP

DRINK FROM A STRAW

UNDRESS THEMSELVES

TAKE TRASH TO THE TRASH CAN

FEED THEMSELVES

CLEAN UP SPILLS

FOLLOW TWO-STEP INSTRUCTIONS

SLEEP IN A TODDLER BED
(most of the time)

HELP FILL A PET'S FOOD DISH

USE THE POTTY
(maybe)

What are some things your two-year-old has worked to accomplish so far?

_____

_____

_____

_____

_____

_____

_____

_____

_____

_____

_____

_____

_____

_____

_____

_____

_____

Letting your two-year-old "do it myself" takes patience—and a lot of wet wipes. How are you allowing for extra time for your toddler to try new things? What do you do to reward their efforts?

What are some things you hope your toddler will be able to do independently in the next phase?

_____

_____

_____

_____

_____

_____

_____

_____

_____

_____

_____

_____

_____

_____

_____

_____

How are you helping them develop those skills now?

_____

_____

_____

_____

_____

_____

_____

_____

_____

_____

_____

_____

_____

_____

_____

_____

_____

EVERY KID

NEEDS

fun

OVER TIME

—

TO GIVE

THEM

connection.

WAYS TO HAVE FUN WITH YOUR TWO-YEAR-OLD

TOYS:

TRUCKS, TRAINS, AND DOLLS

JUMBO CRAYONS

PEG PUZZLES

BEAD MAZES

POUNDING BENCH

MEGA BLOCKS®

RIDING AND SCOOTING TOYS

A SOFT BALL FOR ROLLING AND THROWING

PEG PUZZLES

PLAY-DOH®

FINGER PAINT

PLAY KITCHEN

ALPHABET LETTERS

ACTIVITIES:

GO TO THE PARK

SING "ITSY-BITSY-SPIDER"

BLOW BUBBLES

PUSH A SWING

ROLL A BALL

DO A SILLY DANCE

LET THEM "HIDE"
(Pretend not to notice that 3ft. tall giggling lump behind your curtains.)

What are some activities that make you and your two-year-old laugh?

When are the best times of the day, or week, for you to set aside to have fun with your two-year-old?

What are some ways you want to celebrate the special days coming up this year?

3RD BIRTHDAY

HOLIDAYS

EVERY KID

NEEDS

people

OVER TIME

—

TO GIVE

THEM

belonging.

ADULTS WHO MIGHT INFLUENCE YOUR TWO-YEAR-OLD

PARENTS

PARENT'S FRIENDS

GRANDPARENTS

NURSERY WORKERS

AUNTS AND UNCLES

BABYSITTERS OR NANNIES

List at least five adults who have influence in your two-year-old's life right now.

(?) HINT: They're probably the adults who understand some of your two-year-old's words.

_____

_____

_____

_____

_____

_____

_____

_____

_____

_____

_____

_____

_____

_____

_____

_____

What is one way these adults could help you and your two-year-old this year?

EXAMPLES: pray for you, read to your two-year-old, give your two-year-old an opportunity to play with another kid

_____

_____

_____

_____

_____

_____

_____

_____

_____

_____

_____

_____

_____

_____

_____

_____

_____

What are a few ways you could show these adults appreciation
for the significant role they play in your child's life?

_____

_____

_____

_____

_____

_____

_____

_____

_____

_____

_____

_____

_____

_____

_____

_____

_____

_____

_____

_____

_____

_____

_____

_____

_____

_____

_____

_____

_____

_____

_____

_____

_____

_____

_____

_____

_____

_____

_____

_____

EVERY KID

NEEDS

words

OVER TIME

—

TO GIVE

THEM

direction.

WORDS YOUR TWO-YEAR-OLD NEEDS TO HEAR

Improving your child's vocabulary will help them in the phases to come. Here are a few ways you can help:

1.

Talk to your toddler—the more the better.

2.

Use facial expressions and body language often.

3.

Repeat what they say, and add words. (When they say "truck," you say, "Would you like to play with your truck?")

4.

Give your toddler options. ("Do you want an apple or a banana?")

What word (or words) describe your hopes for your child in this phase?

DETERMINED	MOTIVATED	GENTLE
ENCOURAGING	INTROSPECTIVE	PASSIONATE
SELF-ASSURED	ENTHUSIASTIC	PATIENT
ASSERTIVE	JOYFUL	FORGIVING
DARING	ENTERTAINING	CREATIVE
INSIGHTFUL	INDEPENDENT	WITTY
COMPASSIONATE	OBSERVANT	AMBITIOUS
AMIABLE	SENSITIVE	HELPFUL
EASY-GOING	ENDEARING	AUTHENTIC
DILIGENT	ADVENTUROUS	INVENTIVE
PROACTIVE	HONEST	DEVOTED
OPTIMISTIC	CURIOUS	GENUINE
FEARLESS	DEPENDABLE	ATTENTIVE
AFFECTIONATE	GENEROUS	HARMONIOUS
COURAGEOUS	COMMITTED	EMPATHETIC
CAUTIOUS	RESPONSIBLE	COURAGEOUS
DEVOTED	TRUSTWORTHY	FLEXIBLE
INQUISITIVE	THOUGHTFUL	CAREFUL
PATIENT	LOYAL	NURTURING
OPEN-MINDED	KIND	RELIABLE

Where can you place those words in your home so they will
remind you what you want for your child this year?

_____

_____

_____

_____

_____

_____

_____

_____

_____

_____

_____

_____

_____

_____

_____

_____

Write down some of your two-year-old's first sentences or favorite words. *(At some point this year, try to get a recording of their voice—it will have changed before you know it.)*

_____

_____

_____

_____

_____

_____

_____

_____

_____

_____

_____

_____

_____

_____

_____

_____

SECTION THREE

FOUR CONVERSATIONS

TO HAVE IN THIS

PHASE

WHEN YOU KNOW
WHERE YOU WANT
TO GO,

AND YOU KNOW
WHERE YOU ARE
NOW,

YOU CAN ALWAYS
DO SOMETHING

TO MOVE IN A
BETTER DIRECTION.

OVER THE NEXT 832 WEEKS OF YOUR CHILD'S LIFE, SOME CONVERSATIONS MAY MATTER MORE THAN OTHERS.

WHAT YOU SAY, FOR EXAMPLE, REGARDING . . .	MIGHT HAVE LESS IMPACT ON THEIR FUTURE THAN WHAT YOU SAY REGARDING . . .
Pirates Spiders and Football	Health Sex Technology or Faith.

The next pages are about the conversations that matter most. On the left page is a destination—what you might want to be true in your kid's life 832 weeks from now. On the right page is a goal for conversations with your two-year-old and a few suggestions about what you might want to say.

Healthy habits

—

LEARNING TO
STRENGTHEN
MY BODY THROUGH
EXERCISE, NUTRITION,
AND SELF-ADVOCACY

THIS YEAR YOU WILL

ESTABLISH BASIC NUTRITION

SO YOUR CHILD WILL HAVE CONSISTENT CARE AND EXPERIENCE A VARIETY OF FOOD.

Even though you no longer have pediatric visits every few months, you should schedule a well visit at least once per year. You can also begin to build a foundation of healthy habits for your two-year-old with a few simple words.

SAY THINGS LIKE . . .

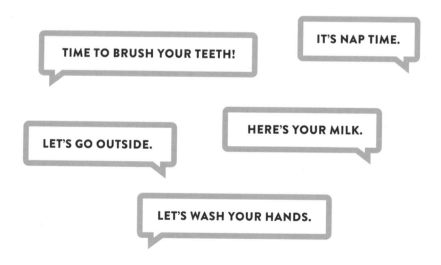

TIME TO BRUSH YOUR TEETH!

IT'S NAP TIME.

LET'S GO OUTSIDE.

HERE'S YOUR MILK.

LET'S WASH YOUR HANDS.

What are your goals for providing your two-year-old with good nutrition and exercise? *(Okay, "exercise" may be a stretch, but running after big kids at the park counts.)*

_____

_____

_____

_____

_____

_____

_____

_____

_____

_____

_____

_____

_____

_____

_____

_____

_____

_____

Who will help you monitor and improve your two-year-old's health this year?

_____

_____

_____

_____

_____

_____

_____

_____

_____

_____

_____

_____

_____

_____

_____

_____

_____

What are your own health goals for this year? How can you improve the habits in your own life—*even in a phase when you might find yourself asking, "Should I eat that mac 'n' cheese they hardly touched?"*

_____

_____

_____

_____

_____

_____

_____

_____

_____

_____

_____

_____

_____

_____

_____

_____

Sexual integrity

—

GUARDING MY
POTENTIAL FOR
INTIMACY THROUGH
APPROPRIATE
BOUNDARIES
AND MUTUAL
RESPECT

THIS YEAR YOU WILL

INTRODUCE THEM TO THEIR BODY

SO YOUR CHILD WILL DISCOVER THEIR BODY
AND DEFINE PRIVACY.

There's a good chance your two-year-old is becoming more aware of their body and the bodies of others. Use this time to lay a foundation for future conversations by simply talking about bodies in a positive way.

SAY THINGS LIKE . . .

> **THAT'S YOUR NOSE. THOSE ARE YOUR EYES. THAT'S YOUR VAGINA / PENIS.**
> (Help your child learn the correct names of body parts—experts suggest that learning proper words can protect your kid from potential harm as well as create a positive view of their body.)

> **NO, GIRLS DON'T HAVE A PENIS.**
> (If your child notices that someone's body is different than their own, talk about the differences.)

What influences shaped your views of sex growing up?

(Examples: parents, media, friends, other adults . . .)

How does your own life story shape your future hopes for your child in this area?

_____

_____

_____

_____

_____

_____

_____

_____

_____

_____

_____

_____

_____

_____

_____

_____

_____

_____

When it comes to your child's sexuality, what do you hope is true for them 832 weeks from now?

Are you and your spouse, or your child's other parent, on the same page when it comes to talking about sex with your child? How might you work on a plan to communicate your hopes, expectations, and real-time conversations with your child about sex?

_____

_____

_____

_____

_____

_____

_____

_____

_____

_____

_____

_____

_____

_____

_____

Technological responsibility

—

LEVERAGING THE POTENTIAL OF ONLINE EXPERIENCES TO ENHANCE MY OFFLINE COMMUNITY AND SUCCESS

THIS YEAR YOU WILL

ENJOY THE ADVANTAGES

SO YOUR CHILD WILL EXPERIENCE BOUNDARIES AND HAVE POSITIVE EXPOSURE.

One advantage to technology is that you probably already have a resident expert who navigates a tablet faster than some adults. But since two-year-olds are drawn to a screen, it's also time to have a few conversations about digital devices.

SAY THINGS LIKE . . .

NO JUICE BY THE COMPUTER.

TABLETS DON'T GO IN THE BATHTUB.

A PHONE IS NOT A HAMMER.

LET'S TURN OFF THE T.V. NOW.
(Two-year-olds don't need to watch a full season of *Sesame Street* in one sitting.)

IS THERE ANYONE OUT THERE WHO CAN RELATE?
(Use technology to connect to other adults.)

What kind of digital access was available to you when you were growing up? How have things changed since then?

_____

_____

_____

_____

_____

_____

_____

_____

_____

_____

_____

_____

_____

_____

_____

_____

_____

_____

What are some issues you think may come up as you raise your child in a digitally connected world? Where can you go to find advice to help navigate those issues?

_____

_____

_____

_____

_____

_____

_____

_____

_____

_____

_____

_____

_____

_____

_____

_____

When it comes to your child's engagement with technology, what do you hope is true for them 832 weeks from now?

_____

_____

_____

_____

_____

_____

_____

_____

_____

_____

_____

_____

_____

_____

_____

_____

_____

What are your own personal values and disciplines when it comes to leveraging technology? Are there ways you want to improve your own savvy, skill, or responsibility in this area?

_____

_____

_____

_____

_____

_____

_____

_____

_____

_____

_____

_____

_____

_____

_____

_____

_____

Authentic faith

—

TRUSTING JESUS IN A WAY THAT TRANSFORMS HOW I LOVE GOD, MYSELF, AND THE REST OF THE WORLD

THIS YEAR YOU WILL

INCITE WONDER

SO YOUR CHILD WILL KNOW GOD'S LOVE
AND MEET GOD'S FAMILY.

Your two-year-old listens to your words. So this phase is the perfect time to begin talking, singing, and reading out loud with your toddler about faith. Begin by simply incorporating faith into your daily routines.

SAY THINGS LIKE . . .

GOD MADE YOU.
GOD LOVES YOU.
JESUS WANTS TO BE YOUR FRIEND FOREVER.

GOD, THANK YOU FOR . . .
GOD, PLEASE HELP US . . .
(Pray aloud while you are with your two-year-old.)

JESUS LOVES ME.
(Sing songs together.)

LET'S READ ABOUT HOW GOD MADE THE WORLD.
LET'S READ ABOUT CHRISTMAS.
LET'S READ ABOUT EASTER.
(Read a few Bible story books—the kind with really good pictures.)

Who will help you develop your child's faith as they grow?

_____

_____

_____

_____

_____

_____

_____

_____

_____

_____

_____

_____

_____

_____

_____

_____

_____

_____

Is there a volunteer at your church who shows up consistently each week for your child? Do you attend a consistent service so your kid knows who will greet them each week?

_____

_____

_____

_____

_____

_____

_____

_____

_____

_____

_____

_____

_____

_____

_____

_____

_____

When it comes to your child's faith, what do you hope is true for them 832 weeks from now?

_____

_____

_____

_____

_____

_____

_____

_____

_____

_____

_____

_____

_____

_____

_____

_____

_____

_____

What routines or habits do you have in your own life that are stretching your faith?

_____

_____

_____

_____

_____

_____

_____

_____

_____

_____

_____

_____

_____

_____

_____

_____

_____

_____

_____

THE

rhythm

OF YOUR

WEEK

—

WILL SHAPE

THE VALUES

IN YOUR

home.

NOW THAT YOU HAVE FILLED THIS BOOK WITH DREAMS, IDEAS, AND GOALS, IT MAY SEEM AS IF YOU WILL NEVER HAVE TIME TO GET IT ALL DONE.

Actually, you have *832 weeks*.

And every week has potential.

The secret to making the most of this phase with your two-year-old is to take advantage of the time you already have. Create a rhythm to your weeks by leveraging these four times together.

Set the mood for the day. Smile. Greet them with words of love.

Reinforce simple ideas. Talk to your toddler and play music as you go.

Be personal. Spend one-on-one time that communicates love and affection.

Wind down together. Provide comfort as the day draws to a close.

What seem to be your two-year-old's best times of the day?

_____

_____

_____

_____

_____

_____

_____

_____

_____

_____

_____

_____

_____

_____

_____

_____

_____

_____

What are some of your favorite routines with your two-year-old?

Write down any other thoughts or questions that you have about parenting your two-year-old.

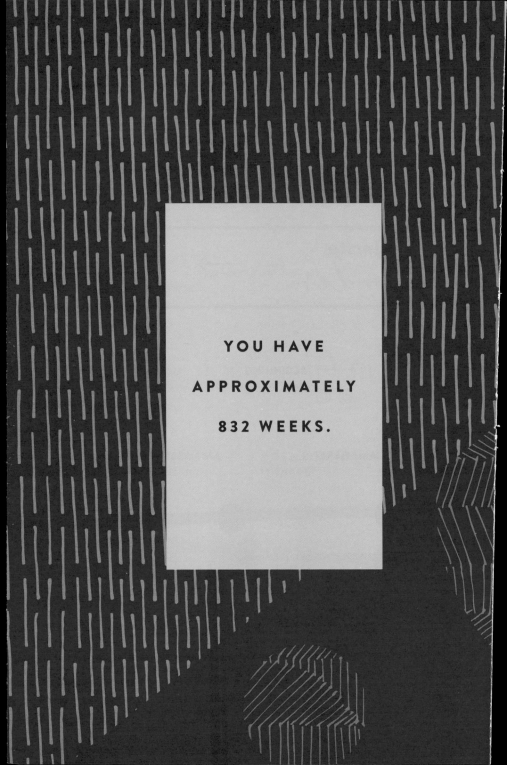

YOU HAVE

APPROXIMATELY

832 WEEKS.

ABOUT THE AUTHORS

KRISTEN IVY @kristen_ivy

Kristen Ivy is executive director of the Phase Project. She and her husband, Matt, are in the preschool and elementary phases with three kids: Sawyer, Hensley, and Raleigh.

Kristen earned her Bachelors of Education from Baylor University in 2004 and received a Master of Divinity from Mercer University in 2009. She worked in the public school system as a high school biology and English teacher, where she learned firsthand the importance of influencing the next generation.

Kristen is also the President at Orange and has played an integral role in the development of the elementary, middle school, and high school curriculum and has shared her experiences at speaking events across the country. She is the co-author of *Playing for Keeps*, *Creating a Lead Small Culture*, *It's Just a Phase*, and *Don't Miss It*.

REGGIE JOINER @reggiejoiner

Reggie Joiner is founder and CEO of the reThink Group and co-founder of the Phase Project. He and his wife, Debbie, have reared four kids into adulthood. They now also have two grandchildren.

The reThink Group (also known as Orange) is a non-profit organization whose purpose is to influence those who influence the next generation. Orange provides resources and training for churches and organizations that create environments for parents, kids, and teenagers.

Before starting the reThink Group in 2006, Reggie was one of the founders of North Point Community Church. During his 11 years with Andy Stanley, Reggie was the executive director of family ministry, where he developed a new concept for relevant ministry to children, teenagers, and married adults. Reggie has authored and co-authored more than 10 books including: *Think Orange, Seven Practices of Effective Ministry, Parenting Beyond Your Capacity, Playing for Keeps, Lead Small, Creating a Lead Small Culture*, and his latest, *A New Kind of Leader* and *Don't Miss It*.

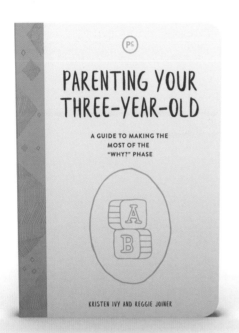

MAKE THE MOST OF EVERY PHASE IN YOUR CHILD'S LIFE

The guide in your hand is one of an eighteen-part series.

So, unless you've figured out a way to freeze time and keep your two-year-old from turning into a three-year-old, you might want to check out the next guide in this set.

Designed in partnership with Parent Cue, each guide will help you rediscover . . .

what's changing about your kid,
the 6 things your kid needs most,
and 4 conversations to have each year.

WANT TO GIFT A FRIEND WITH ALL 18 GUIDES
OR HAVE ALL THE GUIDES ON HAND FOR YOURSELF?

ORDER THE ENTIRE SERIES
OF PHASE GUIDES TODAY.

ORDER NOW AT: WWW.PHASEGUIDES.COM